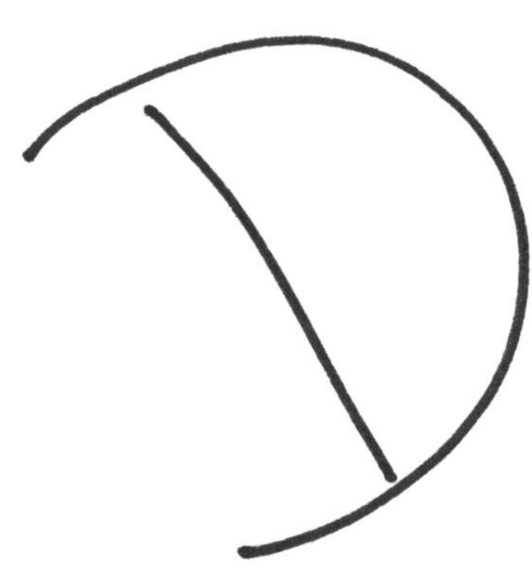

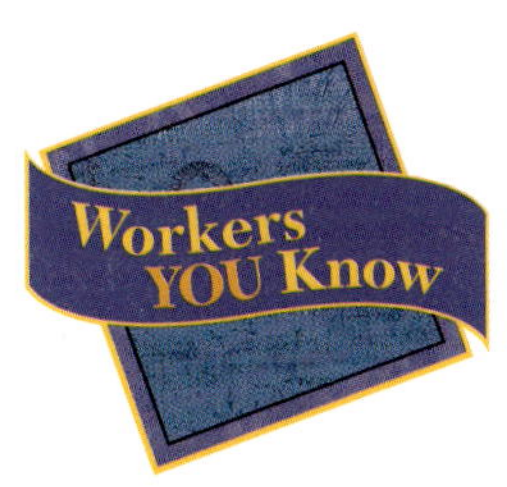

Recreation Director

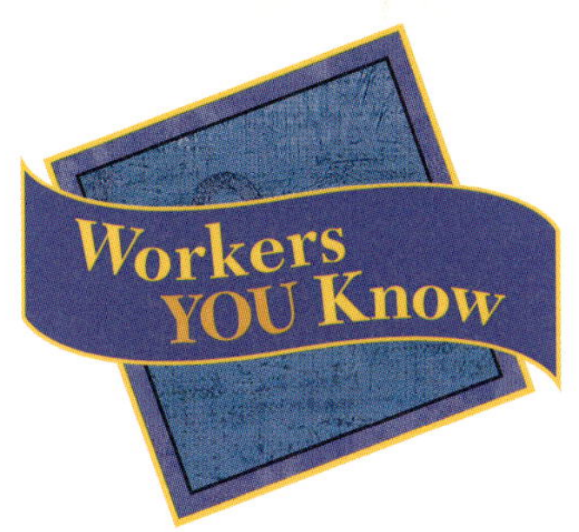

Recreation Director

Kathleen Ermitage

RAINTREE
STECK-VAUGHN
PUBLISHERS

A Harcourt Company

Austin New York
www.steck-vaughn.com

Published by Raintree Steck-Vaughn Publishers,
an imprint of Steck-Vaughn Company

Art Director: Max Brinkmann
Editor: Pam Wells
Design and Illustration: Proof Positive/Farrowlyne Associates, Inc.
Planned and Produced by
Proof Positive/Farrowlyne Associates, Inc.

Library of Congress Cataloging-in-Publication Data

Ermitage, Kathleen.
Recreation director/Kathleen Ermitage.
p. cm. — (Workers you know)
Summary: A recreation director at a city community center tells about his job, which includes planning activities, ordering supplies, working with people of different ages, and more.
ISBN 0–8172–5593–1
1. Recreation leaders—Juvenile literature. 2. Recreation leadership—Juvenile literature. [1. Recreation leadership. 2. Occupations.] I. Title. II. Series.

GV181.4 .E76 2000
790'.023'73—dc21

99–057362

Printed and bound in the United States
1 2 3 4 5 6 7 8 9 0 LB 03 02 01 00

Acknowledgments:
Photo Credits: **29:** © Lawrence Migdale/Tony Stone Images;
32: © Lawrence Migdale/Tony Stone Images

Note: You will find more information about becoming a recreation director on the last page of this book.

For many workers, talking—and working with people—is part of the job. Nurses talk to patients and doctors. Teachers talk to students. Restaurant workers deal with customers and with each other. Secretaries talk to people on the phone, greet them at the door, and work together as part of a team. Construction workers work in teams, too. Police officers talk to each other and with people on the street. And what do I do?

Tom Li

My name is Tom Li. I'm a recreation director. I work at the city community center. I plan activities for people to do together to have fun. All kinds of people, young and old, come to the community center to relax and play. We all share what is here.

This morning, I'm leading a group for toddlers. This is a play group for children under three and their parents or caregivers. The tot group meets in the gym, so before everyone comes, I get ready. I set up mats for running and jungle gyms for climbing. I also get out lots of balls and blocks to play with.

Finally, I turn on some music. We do a lot of singing and dancing in this group. I even set up a table in the corner with some crayons and paper.

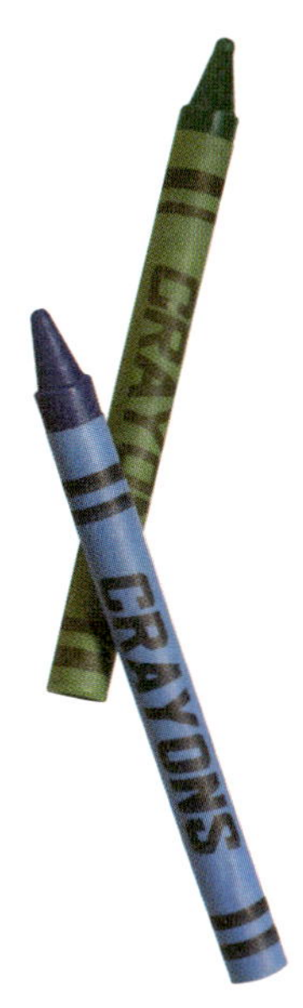

Here comes Eli—he's two. His dad is with him. And there's one-year-old Katherine with her mom. When all the kids arrive, we sit in a circle and sing songs for a few minutes. You might know some of the songs we sing, like "Row, Row, Row Your Boat." We also do nursery rhymes, like "Hickory, Dickory, Dock." I've been teaching the kids hand motions to go with the songs and nursery rhymes. I show them how to make their hands twinkle like stars, run like mice, or open and shut like the doors on a bus.

After we sing songs, I usually tell the kids a story. Sometimes I bring a book to read, but at other times I make up the story. I bring puppets, toys, and pictures with me to help get the kids interested. I really like this part of my day because I can use what I learned in school—music, language, and drama.

After our circle time, the kids and I work on a craft project. We color with crayons, and sometimes we cut out and glue things together. Then, we have a snack after we finish our work. The adults take turns bringing snacks, so that's one thing I don't have to worry about.

I save the artwork and post it on the bulletin board in the lobby of the community center. Everyone likes to see what the kids have been working on.

Now the tots are ready to run around and play! They do a lot of climbing. We have a safe space for them to run and jump and climb. But I watch them closely anyway.

I don't spend all day working with people. Some of the time I work in the office of the community center, where I can do some thinking and planning. It's my job to think of fun things for everyone in the community to do.

A few days ago I went to see Davita, my boss, with a new idea. Some of the people in the neighborhood have to use wheelchairs to get around. So now I'm planning a new program—Basketball on Wheels.

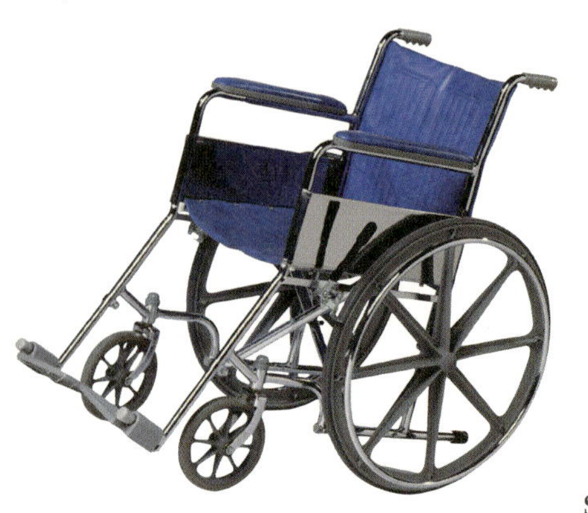

I think Basketball on Wheels is a great idea, but it takes a lot of planning. I use the Internet to find out about other wheelchair basketball groups around the country. Then I write to the leaders to find out if they use the same rules as the ones that are used for regular basketball. I also ask them if we need any special equipment. If we do need special equipment, I will have to find out how much it costs and order it.

Davita will let me know how much we have to spend. I will need things like equipment and color copies of the posters kids have drawn. We will sell the posters at the game. I also have to use math and problem-solving skills to see if we can afford the new equipment.

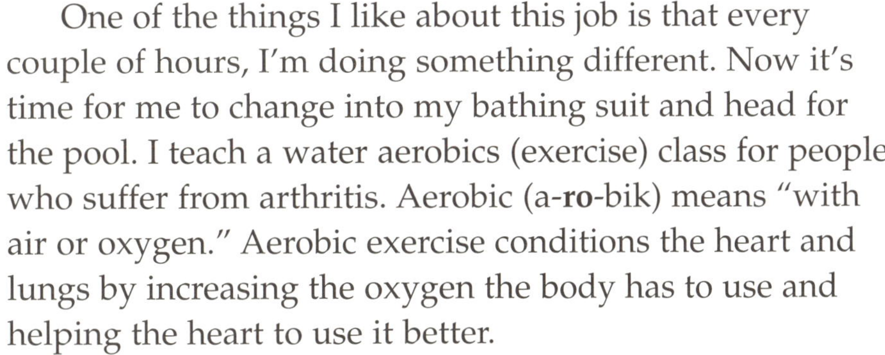

One of the things I like about this job is that every couple of hours, I'm doing something different. Now it's time for me to change into my bathing suit and head for the pool. I teach a water aerobics (exercise) class for people who suffer from arthritis. Aerobic (a-**ro**-bik) means "with air or oxygen." Aerobic exercise conditions the heart and lungs by increasing the oxygen the body has to use and helping the heart to use it better.

People with arthritis have a lot of pain in their joints, like their knuckles, knees, and hips. Sometimes exercise can help prevent arthritis from getting worse. It also helps people with arthritis to stay healthy and feel better. Exercising in water doesn't hurt painful joints as much as exercising on land.

Davita asked me to teach the water aerobics class because she knows that I used to be a lifeguard. I had to get special training to teach this class, though. I learned a lot of science, mostly about how the human body works. I learned ways people with arthritis can move in water to protect their joints. When I teach the class, I am careful not to include any activities that are likely to hurt people's joints. I also do different exercises for each body part.

When we plan classes at the community center, we try to think about what times of day are best for different groups of people. The water aerobics class is at noon, because people like to work out on their lunch hours. And the tots' class is early because children under three often nap in the afternoon.

Soon it will be time for the community center's after-school program. The community center is right next to an elementary school, so it is a safe place for kids to play until their parents can pick them up after work. They play games, write stories, and do crafts.

I think the weather will be nice today, so I am planning a soccer game. We can play in a big field next to the community center. First, though, I have to check and make sure we have all the equipment we need for the game.

As long as I'm here checking the soccer supplies, I might as well check all the supplies. Part of my job is to make sure we have enough equipment for all the activities people do at the community center. I have a list that shows all the supplies we should have. If we are low on some, it's my job to order more.

I also check to make sure the supplies and equipment are in good condition. Everything wears out in time. Sometimes the flags we use for flag football get worn out. So we have to replace them.

It looks like we have plenty of equipment for soccer. And it's in pretty good condition, so the game is on!

I got my equipment out just in time. Here are Gwen and Joel. They've played soccer with me before, so they know how to set up the equipment. I hand Gwen and Joel a soccer ball and some nets. Then, I ask them to set everything up on the field.

As the other kids arrive, I pass out shin guards. These protect the front part of the leg below the knee and above the ankle. After everyone has put on the shin guards, we practice kicking, dribbling, and passing.

I never know how many kids will show up each day. I just try to make sure each team has the same number of players. That way, the game will be fair.

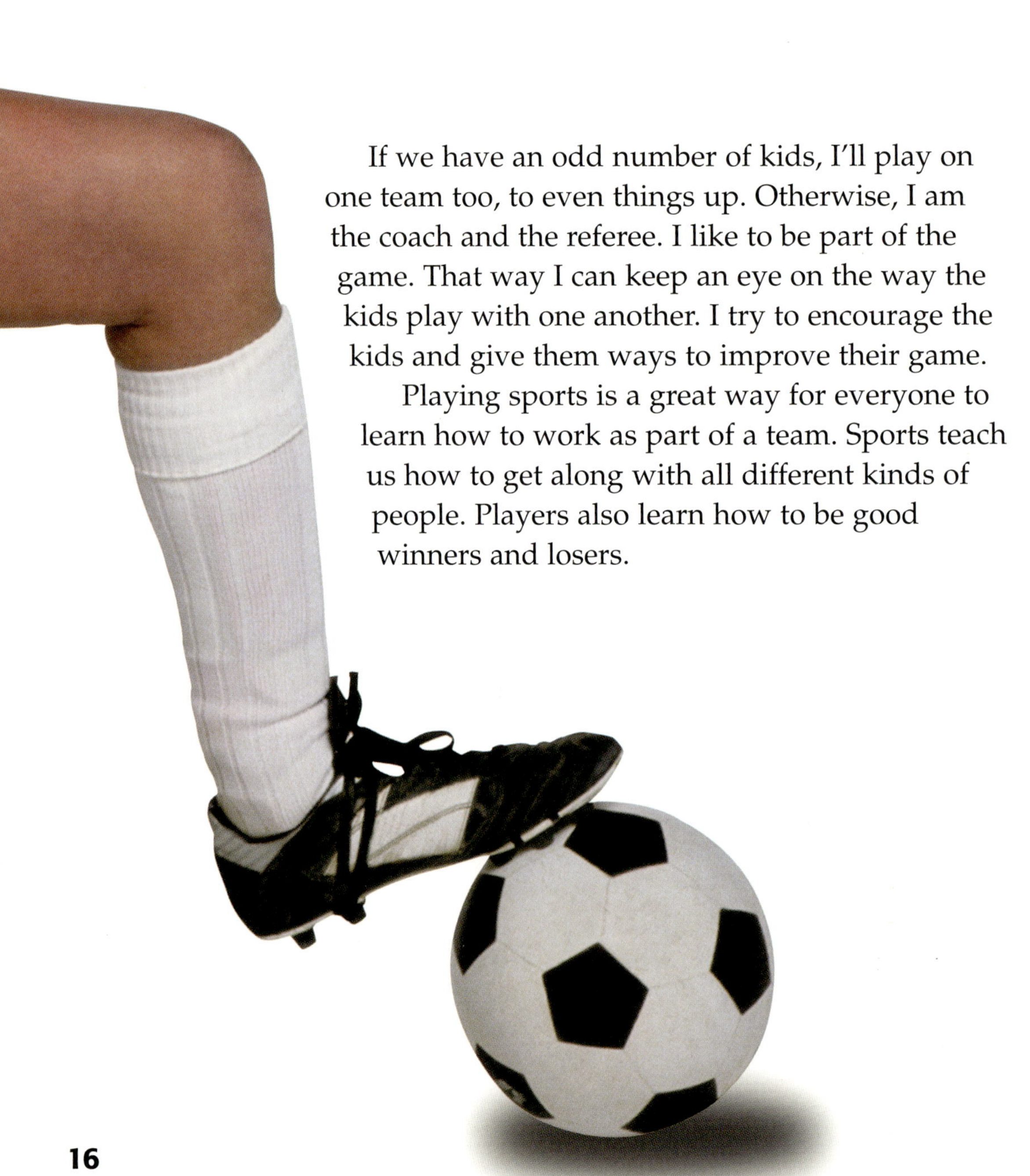

If we have an odd number of kids, I'll play on one team too, to even things up. Otherwise, I am the coach and the referee. I like to be part of the game. That way I can keep an eye on the way the kids play with one another. I try to encourage the kids and give them ways to improve their game.

Playing sports is a great way for everyone to learn how to work as part of a team. Sports teach us how to get along with all different kinds of people. Players also learn how to be good winners and losers.

The game is going well. Everyone seems to be having a great time. But the sky is growing very dark. I can hear the rumble of thunder in the distance.

I pass the ball to Gwen. She starts to run, kicking the ball as she goes.

Wait a minute! I hear Joel shouting for me. Gwen has been hurt.

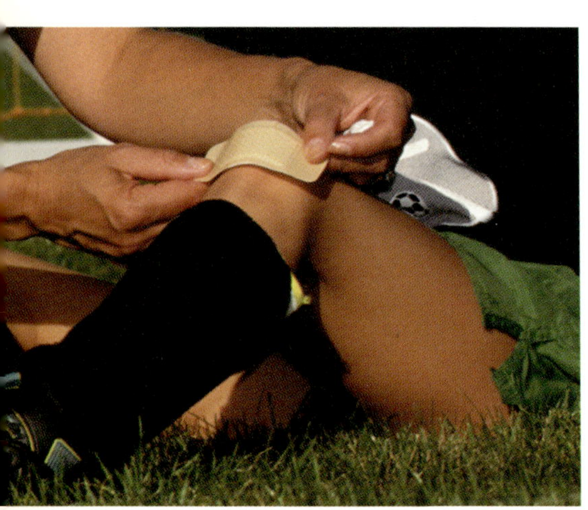

If someone gets hurt, I know what to do. I learned about first aid when I was in school and am allowed to practice it. First aid is emergency medical treatment given to injured or sick people before professional medical care arrives. Accidents can happen, no matter how careful we are. This is why it is important for me to know first aid and to have my kit ready.

I hear another rumble of thunder. The storm is getting closer. I run to grab my first-aid kit from the sideline. Then I run over to Gwen and Joel.

My first-aid kit has bandages, tape, and scissors for covering up cuts. It has skin wipes for cleaning cuts. It also has a cold pack to keep down any swelling. I keep my first-aid kit close by. I have to be prepared. When the kids are at the park with me, I take good care of them.

I ask Gwen to bend her knee for me. She bends it slowly, but I can tell it hurts. First, I clean the cut and put a bandage on it. Then, I put on a cold pack.

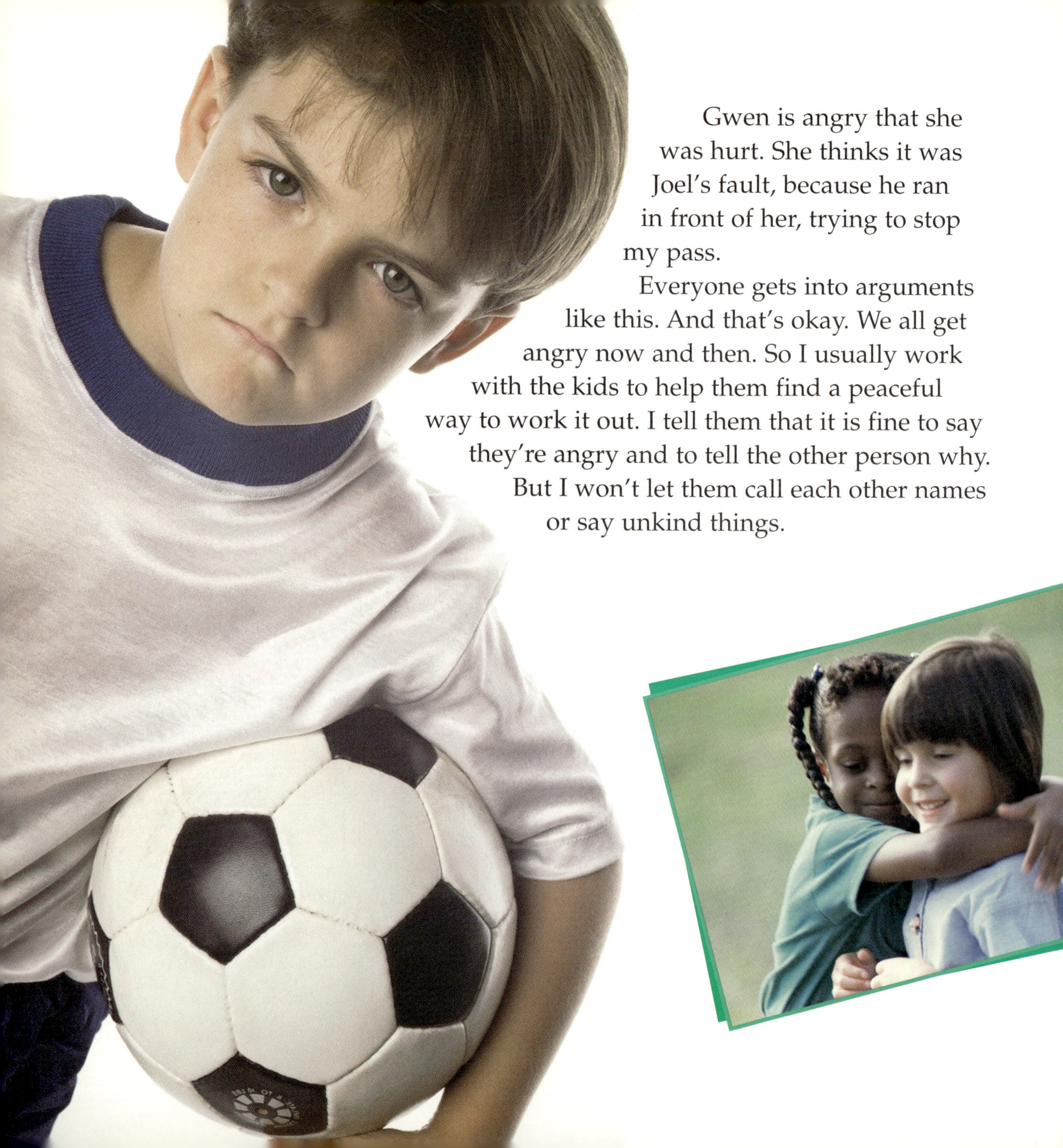

Gwen is angry that she was hurt. She thinks it was Joel's fault, because he ran in front of her, trying to stop my pass.

Everyone gets into arguments like this. And that's okay. We all get angry now and then. So I usually work with the kids to help them find a peaceful way to work it out. I tell them that it is fine to say they're angry and to tell the other person why. But I won't let them call each other names or say unkind things.

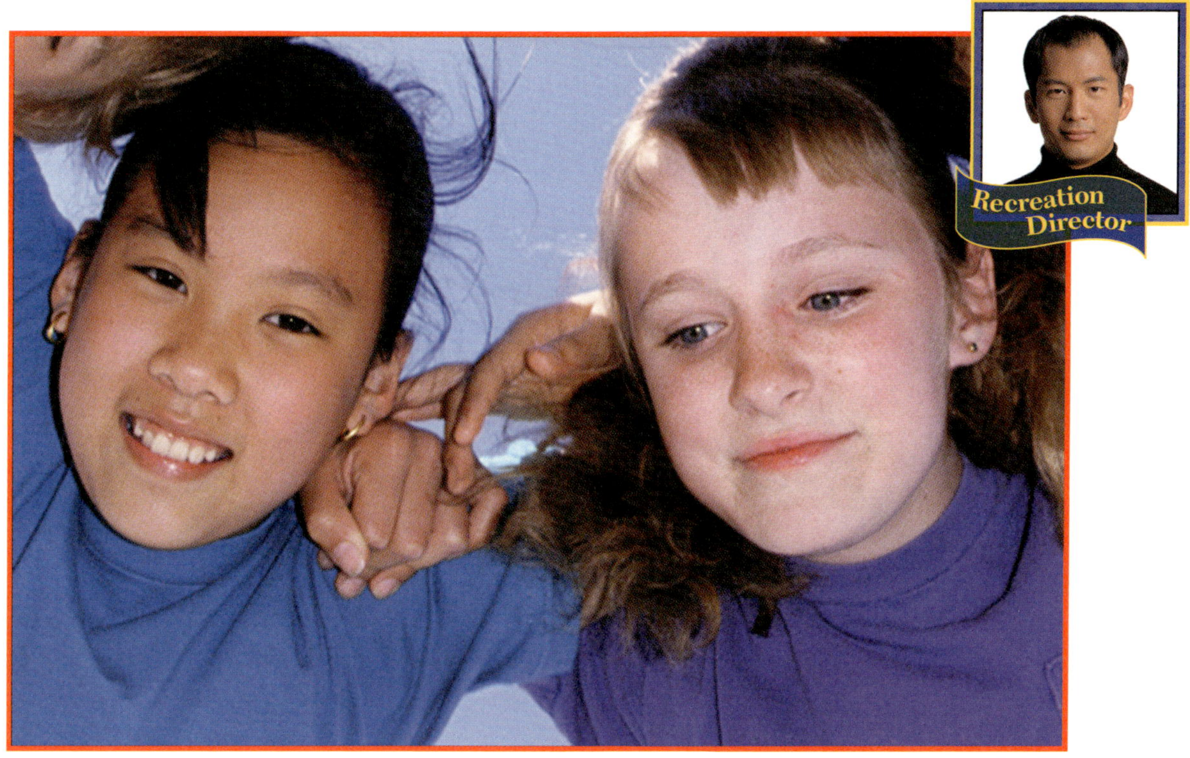

I know it will be hard for Gwen to be fair to Joel while her knee still hurts. So I will help her. I ask Joel if he meant to hurt Gwen. He explains that it was an accident. Then I ask Joel to help Gwen into the community center, so she can rest her knee.

Gwen and Joel frown at each other. Then, Gwen leans on Joel's shoulder. They limp off together. I hope they'll talk more about what happened. Gwen needs to know that what happened was an accident. But Joel should realize that he should have watched where he was going. I will check with them later.

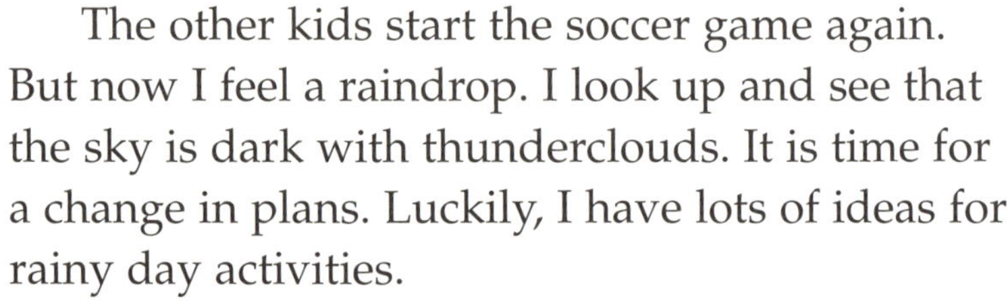

The other kids start the soccer game again. But now I feel a raindrop. I look up and see that the sky is dark with thunderclouds. It is time for a change in plans. Luckily, I have lots of ideas for rainy day activities.

Inside the community center, I hand out paper and pencils. I explain to the group that they will be writing stories. But they will still be working together.

Each person will write one or two sentences on a sheet of paper. Next, each one will pass the paper to the person on the right, who will continue the story. They will keep passing the papers around until the papers that they had started come back to them. Finally, they can take turns reading the stories aloud. If there is time, they can draw colorful pictures to go with the stories.

While the kids are writing, I have my own writing to do. Every time someone gets hurt in one of my groups, I have to write a report about it. I fill out a form explaining what happened, who was hurt, and what I did to help. Today, I will have to write a report explaining how Gwen got hurt.

I will give the report to my boss, Davita. She looks at all the injury reports and decides whether we need to do anything to make the community center safer. If she thinks I could have done something to stop an accident from happening, she will tell me. We are very serious about safety around here!

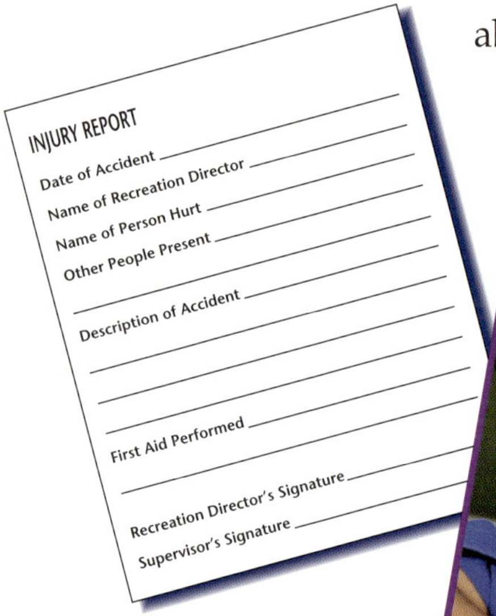

INJURY REPORT

Date of Accident ________

Name of Recreation Director ________

Name of Person Hurt ________

Other People Present ________

Description of Accident ________

First Aid Performed ________

Recreation Director's Signature ________

Supervisor's Signature ________

After I finish writing my report, I pack up the soccer supplies. Everyone helps bring the supplies inside. The kids are great about helping me keep our park clean.

I wave at another recreation director. José brought his group inside, too. He works with elderly people. In order to work well with them, José has to know what elderly people like to do, and what they can do. Just as I have to learn about the bodies and minds of children, he has to learn about older people's bodies and minds.

José

I let my group pass the stories around for a while. I see them drawing pictures. Then, I ask them to share their stories with each other. They take turns reading the stories aloud. These kids are great writers! They love hearing the stories because everyone wrote part of every story.

Writing stories is just one of the activities we can do at the community center on a rainy day. Sometimes we do craft projects—just like the tots did, only a little more complicated. One day we made kites. Another time we made holiday decorations for the community center. We also play games, like checkers, backgammon, and chess. Sometimes we dress up and do skits or put on puppet shows. I always try to think of activities that will be fun for everyone.

When the kids finish reading their stories to each other, I will post them on the bulletin board in the community center. That bulletin board is getting very crowded! But I love to show off the work the kids do. I ask everyone to help put away the paper and crayons—all except for Joel and Gwen. I want to talk to them. I ask if they need to talk any more about the accident. I don't want them to leave the community center still feeling angry at each other. Gwen and Joel tell me that they have worked things out on their own. I thought they would!

At the end of the day, parents and caregivers arrive. I check my list of the kids in the program and make sure that I have seen each child leave with an adult. Sometimes parents are late, and I stay with the kids until their parents come.

When Gwen's father comes to pick her up, I explain to him that Gwen had an accident. I tell him that I was sorry it happened, but that I think Gwen is okay. I explain to him what first-aid treatment I gave her. But I suggest that if her knee continues to hurt, he should take Gwen to see a doctor. On her way out the door, Gwen waves good-bye to Joel. It makes me feel wonderful when kids start out arguing and then end up working out their problems.

The kids have gone home, but my day isn't over yet. Remember Basketball on Wheels? Davita has planned for it to start next month. I'll have to do a lot to get ready.

One of the most important things I have to do is find people who want to join the games, so I have to spread the news about the program. I'll hang posters in the grocery stores and in the schools. I'll also call the newspapers and ask them to add this program to their list of events.

You may be wondering how I got this job. First, I worked summers as a lifeguard and camp counselor. But I had to finish a college degree in physical education before I could get this job. I also had to be trained in first aid and CPR. CPR is a way to help people if they stop breathing or if their hearts stop beating. My lifeguard training helped me to get this job, too.

But all of my education wasn't enough. When my boss hired me, she said that she thought I was very creative. In this job, you have to think of new things to do every day. You also have to be good at solving problems. But most of all, you have to like working with people.

When you work as a recreation director, there are so many different ways to have fun! I know a lot about recreation, but I am going to school to learn even more. I am learning more about the needs of special groups of people, so that I can plan more programs like the water aerobics class and Basketball on Wheels. Soon, I will receive a certificate, or special paper, from the National Parks and Recreation Association (NPRA). I will be a Certified Leisure Professional. That's a fancy way of saying that I plan to be doing this kind of work for a long, long time!

For More Information About Becoming a Recreation Director, Contact:

National Parks and Recreation Association
2775 South Quincy Street, Suite 300
Arlington, VA 22206

National Employee Services and Recreation Association
2211 York Road, Suite 207
Oakbrook, IL 60521-2371

Recreation Director Education, Training, and Requirements:

Most recreation directors have college degrees in Physical Education, Leisure Activities, Fine Arts, or Performing Arts. Most programs require that recreation directors be fully trained in first aid and CPR. Some recreation directors must have drivers' licenses so that they can drive kids to events. They may have to own cars. Other recreation directors work with the elderly in retirement communities or special hospitals. Training programs vary.

Related Careers:

Lifeguard
Camp Counselor
Teacher
Coach